the Boys' Summer book

PSS!

PRICE STERN SLOAN

An Imprint of Penguin Group (USA) Inc.

Written by Guy Campbell
Illustrated by Paul Moran

Cover illustrated by Nikalas Catlow

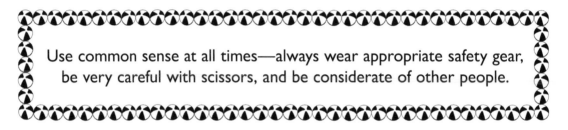

Use common sense at all times—always wear appropriate safety gear,
be very careful with scissors, and be considerate of other people.

PRICE STERN SLOAN
Published by the Penguin Group
Penguin Group (USA) Inc., 375 Hudson Street, New York, New York 10014, USA
Penguin Group (Canada), 90 Eglinton Avenue East, Suite 700,
Toronto, Ontario M4P 2Y3, Canada
(a division of Pearson Penguin Canada Inc.)
Penguin Books Ltd., 80 Strand, London WC2R 0RL, England
Penguin Group Ireland, 25 St. Stephen's Green, Dublin 2, Ireland
(a division of Penguin Books Ltd.)
Penguin Group (Australia), 250 Camberwell Road, Camberwell, Victoria 3124, Australia
(a division of Pearson Australia Group Pty. Ltd.)
Penguin Books India Pvt. Ltd., 11 Community Centre,
Panchsheel Park, New Delhi—110 017, India
Penguin Group (NZ), 67 Apollo Drive, Rosedale, North Shore 0632, New Zealand
(a division of Pearson New Zealand Ltd.)
Penguin Books (South Africa) (Pty.) Ltd., 24 Sturdee Avenue,
Rosebank, Johannesburg 2196, South Africa
Penguin Books Ltd., Registered Offices:
80 Strand, London WC2R 0RL, England

ISBN 978-0-8431-9852-2   10 9 8 7 6 5 4 3 2

CONTENTS

SUMMER SPACE GETAWAY

Take a trip to the puzzle planet for a summer that is out of this world.
All the answers are on page 92.

SPOT THE FLUGROVIAN

Can you spot the Flugrovian within this bunch of alien critters? Flugrovians have five eyes, but no tail. They have some hair on their heads, but no wings. They are also very, very smelly—but luckily you can't tell that from the picture.

SPACE ZOO

Human beings aren't the only animals to venture into space. Animals have been sent into space for over sixty years. The first to go into space were fruit flies in 1947, followed by a monkey named Albert in 1949. Eight years later, a dog named Laika was sent up by the Russians. Since then, lots of animals have been sent into orbit including ants, frogs, mice, rats, and even fish.

Fill this rocket with animals.

4

CRYSTAL CAPER

To fix your damaged spacecraft, you need to get a crystal from the cave. You have a crystal-seeking pig to help you. On your way to the crystal, if your path is blocked by pig-eating cats, you can't pass, but you can pass the crystal-munching dogs.

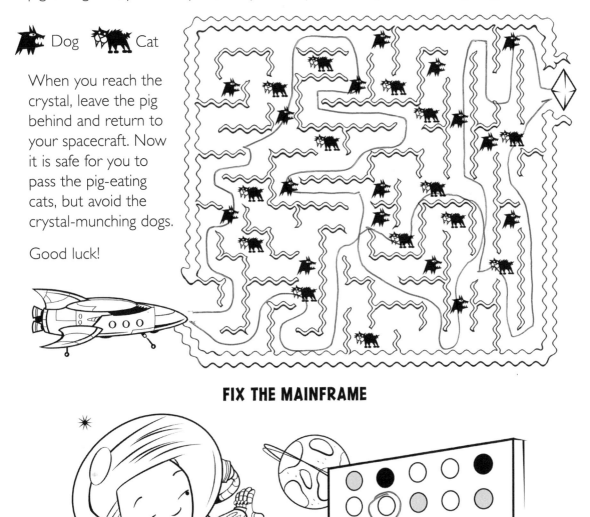

Dog   Cat

When you reach the crystal, leave the pig behind and return to your spacecraft. Now it is safe for you to pass the pig-eating cats, but avoid the crystal-munching dogs.

Good luck!

FIX THE MAINFRAME

Can you put the crystal in the right socket and fix the ship? Choose very carefully.

The crystal must be put in a white socket in a row with two gray sockets and in a column with two black sockets.

MAKE YOUR OWN POWERBOAT

Why not take up powerboat racing this summer? Make your very own high-speed powerboat to race across your bathtub or a pool.

You will need:

an empty plastic tub • a balloon • a rubber band • a bendy straw • scissors • modeling clay

1. Cut the straw in half and keep the bendy end. This will be the exhaust pipe for your boat's "engine."

2. Pull the neck of the balloon over the drinking end of the straw, so that it reaches one inch before the beginning of the bend. Secure it with a rubber band.

3. Place a lump of modeling clay on the outside of your tub toward the bottom-center of one of the narrower ends.

4. Using the point of your scissors, carefully push through from the inside of your tub into the modeling clay. (Ask an adult to help you with this.) Make the hole just big enough for your straw to fit through.

5. Remove the modeling clay and push the straw through the hole so that the balloon is inside the tub.

6. Press some modeling clay onto the inside bottom of the tub. This will help to sink the straw below the surface of the water and make it go faster.

7. Squash some more modeling clay onto the outside of your tub, around where your straw pokes through. This will hold the straw in place and make a seal to stop water from getting into your boat.

8. Your boat is almost ready to race. Blow through the straw to inflate the balloon until it fills the tub. Cover the end of the straw with your thumb to stop the air from escaping.

9. To start your powerboat, place it on the surface of the water and uncover the end of the straw to let the air escape. Watch it speed away.

ANCHORS AWAY!

Can you find which anchor belongs to which boat in this moored maze?
Check your answers on page 92.

AWESOME ANIMAL QUIZ

Answer the questions below to test you and your friends' knowledge of all things animal. Write each player's answers—A, B, C, or D—on the scorecard on the opposite page. All the answers are on page 92.

1. Which furry, hopping animal has a fluffy tail and lucky feet?
- A. Rabbit
- B. Kangaroo
- C. Lemur
- D. Badger

2. Which animal takes part in the sports of show jumping and polo?
- A. Camel
- B. Horse
- C. Dog
- D. Reindeer

3. On which of the following are you most likely to find a polar bear?
- A. Sand
- B. Ice
- C. A bicycle
- D. A television

4. Which country's people take their nickname from the kiwi bird?
- A. Wales
- B. New Zealand
- C. Egypt
- D. France

5. What kind of animal is boy wizard Harry Potter's pet, Hedwig?
- A. Rat
- B. Cat
- C. Toad
- D. Owl

6. Which cat is the fastest land mammal on the planet?
- A. Lion
- B. Tabby
- C. Cheetah
- D. Tiger

7. Which is the biggest land-based animal in the world?
- A. Field mouse
- B. Donkey
- C. Hippopotamus
- D. Elephant

8. Which bird is also the name of a piece on a chessboard?
- A. Rook
- B. Emu
- C. Flamingo
- D. Toucan

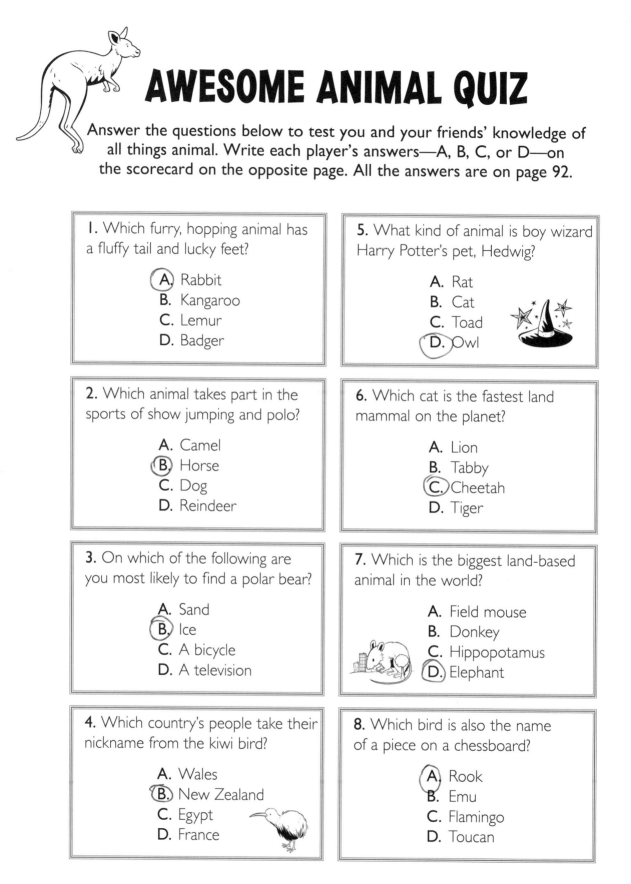

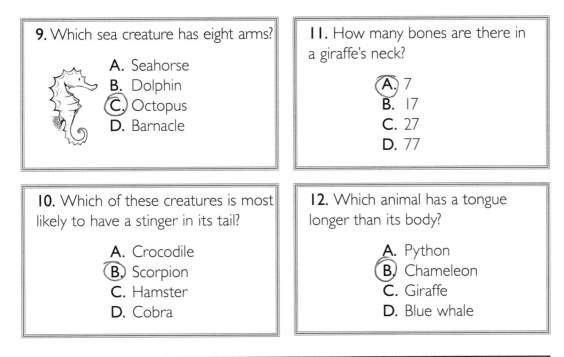

9. Which sea creature has eight arms?

    A. Seahorse
    B. Dolphin
    C. Octopus
    D. Barnacle

11. How many bones are there in a giraffe's neck?

    A. 7
    B. 17
    C. 27
    D. 77

10. Which of these creatures is most likely to have a stinger in its tail?

    A. Crocodile
    B. Scorpion
    C. Hamster
    D. Cobra

12. Which animal has a tongue longer than its body?

    A. Python
    B. Chameleon
    C. Giraffe
    D. Blue whale

Question	Player One	Player Two	Player Three	Player Four
1				
2				
3				
4				
5				
6				
7				
8				
9				
10				
11				
12				
TOTAL SCORE				

THE "HOUSE OF CARDS" CHALLENGE

Give boredom the boot this summer and become a master builder with this "house of cards" challenge.

CHALLENGE ONE:
The Trestle

The basic card house is made by leaning two cards against each other so they make a tall triangle. Put two triangles side by side and gently place another card flat on top. This is a trestle—the building block of a house of cards.

Tip: Building with cards is much easier on a carpet than on a hard floor.

CHALLENGE TWO:
The Great Pyramid

Put two card trestles side by side and link them together by placing another card to overlap where the roofs meet. Build another trestle next to this one, overlapping the roofs as before. To build another floor, build another trestle carefully on top. You will need a steady hand for this.

Keep adding to your pyramid until it falls down or you run out of cards!

CHALLENGE THREE:
Deck Domino Race

Have you ever lined up dominoes and then knocked them all over? It is even more fun with cards! Line up triangles of cards, close enough together so that when you push one over, the next triangle will fall, and the next, and the next. If you have a lot of cards, you can make a long, long line of them.

If you and a friend set up lines or "tracks" the same length, you can race. Prepare your tracks, then push the first triangle over and see whose track tumbles all the way to the end the fastest!

Tip: If you are making a very long line, leave a gap every two feet so that if a card triangle accidentally falls, it won't take out your whole track. When your lines are finished, go back and fill in the gaps.

CHALLENGE FOUR:
The Colosseum of Rome

The Colosseum in Rome, Italy, is a giant stone building built over a thousand years ago. It took many men many years to construct. You can build your own Colosseum out of cards much faster, but you will need lots of cards. See if you can pick up some old packs in thrift stores or at yard sales.

To build your Colosseum, make a circle of trestles about two feet across. To make your circle more stable, overlap the roofs of your trestles with more cards. Once you have built this and it is quite stable, add your next floor on

top. If you have lots of cards, make your ground floor circle bigger than two feet across. If you aren't sure if you have enough cards, start with a smaller circle and add as many floors as you can.

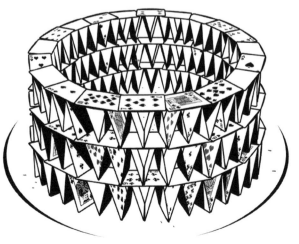

PENS AT THE READY

Whether you are on a long car ride or waiting at the airport, be sure to keep a pen and paper handy for games—time will fly.

BOXING MATCH

You will need two players for this game. To begin, draw a grid of dots on your page measuring seven dots by seven dots like the one shown below.

Take turns drawing a single line that connects two dots. The line must be either horizontal or vertical— no diagonal lines allowed.

The aim of the game is to complete more boxes than your opponent. When it's your turn, if you find three lines around a box, you can finish it twith your line and make it yours. Stake your claim by writing the first letter of your name inside. Each time a player completes a box, he can take another turn.

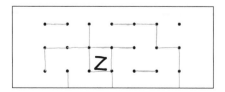

When all the dots have been connected, count how many boxes each player has. The person with the most wins.

Z	Z	Z	Z	Z	S
Z	Z	Z	Z	Z	S
S	S	Z	Z	Z	Z
S	S	Z	Z	Z	S
S	S	Z	Z	S	S
S	S	Z	Z	S	S

Tip: Why not play a really long game with a board measuring twenty dots by twenty dots?

BOX CLEVER

Can you find a place to draw your line that doesn't allow your opponent to complete a square?

Check your answer on page 92.

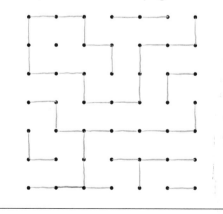

CRAZY SUMMER CONSEQUENCES

You will need two or more players for this game. Each player needs a piece of paper and a pen.

To begin, each player must draw a funny head in the top quarter of his page. The head can be of anything or anyone you like, but don't let anyone see what you are drawing.

When you have finished your drawing, fold down your paper to cover over the head, leaving just the two lines of the neck showing. Swap drawings with another player and draw a body and arms onto the neck in the next quarter of the page. Again, don't let anyone see. Fold your paper over your drawing

as you did before and pass your paper on to the next player for them to draw the bottom half of the body and the legs. Pass your picture on again and draw the feet.

When you have drawn the feet of your crazy creation, pass on your paper and take turns unfolding your picture to reveal the funny figure.

A FLICK TO THE FINISH

You will need two players, a piece of paper, and two different colored felt-tip pens for this game.

Hold the felt-tip pen vertically with one finger on the end and the tip resting on the paper. Press down with your finger and make the pen flick off, making a line on the paper like this:

This is your starting line. Draw a racetrack that begins and ends at the starting line, like the one shown here.

Place your felt-tip pen on the starting line and flick it as you did before, following the direction of the racetrack.

Take turns flicking the pen, placing it at the end of your previous line.

The first player to make it back to the starting line wins!

BECOME A SUMMER SUPERSLEUTH

Get a group of friends together to play these great games
where detectives and criminals duke it out!

THE TONGUE OF TERROR

You will need at least four players for this game.

Choose one person to be the detective and ask him to leave the room. While he is gone, decide together who is going to be the murderer. Ask the detective to come back in.

The murderer then has to "kill" as many people as he can by sticking his tongue out at them without the detective catching him. Each victim must immediately die a dramatic death.

If the murderer manages to kill everyone without the detective catching him, he wins. If the detective names the killer before everyone is dead, he wins!

THE USUAL SUSPECTS

You will need at least five players for this game, a bag, and a pen and piece of paper for each player.

Ask each player to write down the answers to the following questions: "What is your favorite food?," "What is your favorite movie?," "What color is your hair?," "What color are your socks?," and other similar questions. Put all the answer sheets into a bag and then ask one player to be the detective.

The detective must choose a piece of paper from the bag and say: "The suspect matches the following description." He then reads each item on the list one at a time. The first person to guess the identity of the suspect wins and gets to be the detective for the next round.

TOUGH QUESTIONS

You will need at least four players for this game, a pen, and a piece of paper.

Write the word *killer* on a piece of paper. Choose one person to be the detective and send him/her out of the room. Now, decide who is going to be the killer. Give that person the piece of paper to hold in his hand. The detective returns and has to ask three questions to discover who the killer is. The questions must be directed at one player and can only have *yes* or *no* answers. So the detective might ask, ''Tom, does the killer have blond hair?'' After asking all three questions, the detective then has to accuse one of the players of being the killer. The accused player has to open his hands. If he has the paper, the detective wins, and the killer becomes the new detective. If the detective is wrong, he has to go again.

Players cannot lie, but they should try their hardest not to give away the killer's identity.

INVESTIGATE THE CRIME SCENE

This hotel room has been robbed. Study the photograph of the crime scene below for thirty seconds and then answer the questions on the next page. Try to give the police as much information as you can.

INVESTIGATE THE CRIME SCENE CONTINUED . . .

Answer the questions below without turning back to look at the picture on page 15. Check your answers on page 92.

1. When was the photograph taken?

   (A) During the day
   B. At night

2. There are two pictures hanging on the wall. What are they of?

   Eyes. World

3. Where is the soccer ball?

   On pillow

4. Where is the backpack?

   Beside the racket

5. Is the backpack open or closed?

   Closed

6. One of the patio doors is broken. Is it the door on the right or the left?

   Right

7. Where is the broken glass?

   (A) Inside the room
   B. On the patio

8. How many tennis rackets are there in the room?

   ONE

9. Is the suitcase open or closed?

   OPEN

10. Which drawer has been removed from the chest of drawers?

    (A) Top
    B. Middle
    C. Bottom

FIND THE MISSING NUMBER

Each animal in this grid represents a number—either 1, 2, 3, or 4.

If you add up the numbers in any row or column, you get the total at the end of that row or column.

For example, three elephants and a tiger equals 5, and two elephants, a tiger, and a lion equals 8.

Figure out which animal represents which number, and then find the missing number.

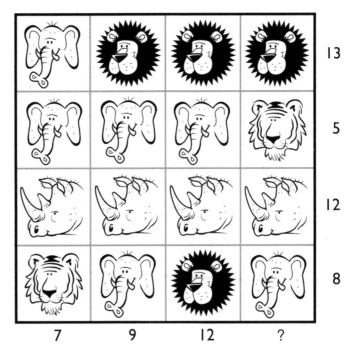

SUMMER SAFARI

What has the explorer discovered in the rainforest?

PUZZLE PARK

The sun's out and you've got a whole day of fun ahead
at Puzzle Park. Check your answers on page 93.

SWINGS AND MERRY-GO-ROUNDS

Each of these circles represents a fun
thing to do at the park. The letters
represent people.

Where the circles cross over one
another, the people like to do more
than one thing. For example, D likes the
merry-go-round and lying on the grass,
but does not like the slide or the swings.

Can you spot who loves the slide and
the swings but does not like the merry-
go-round or lying on the grass?

J and M

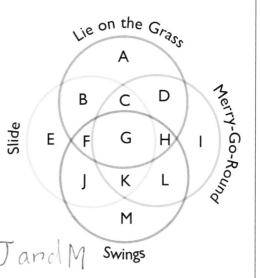

SMOOTHIES AT THE PARK CAFÉ

Can you unscramble the flavors of the smoothies on the café's board?
Which flavor is different from the rest?

Chocolate

MENU

NGOARE

NBAAAN *Banana*

PRABSYRER *Strawberry*

RWSARRETBY *R...*

HLOOATGEG *Chocolate*

EAHPC *Peach*

NUT CRACKERS

Only two of these pictures of a squirrel with his lunch are exactly the same.

Can you find the matching pair?

C & H

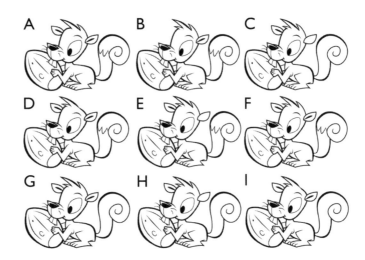

TIME TO GO, TOMMY!

Can you find Tommy and tell him it is time to go home?
Tommy is wearing shorts and gloves but he isn't wearing a hat.
He has on a long-sleeved T-shirt. Can you find him?

SEASIDE CHEF SCHOOL

You're "shore" to like these delicious recipes.

OCTOPASTA PERFECTION

These wriggling octopuses are really delicious and very easy to make. Here's how to make enough to feed two hungry sailors.

You will need:

- 1/2 lb dried spaghetti
- 8 hot dogs
- a pinch of salt
- a pan of boiling water
- 1 small jar tomato sauce
- 2 tablespoons grated cheese

1. Open the package of hot dogs. Chop each of the hot dogs into five equally sized pieces using a butter knife and then put them aside.

2. Break the strands of spaghetti in half.

3. Push eight strands of spaghetti about halfway into each of the hot dog pieces so that the spaghetti is firmly attached.

4. Ask an adult to put them, and the rest of the spaghetti, into a large pot of boiling water with the salt.

5. Boil the spaghetti and hot dogs together following the instructions on the package.

6. When the spaghetti is cooked, ask an adult to drain it very carefully using a colander. Put the colander aside.

7. Heat the sauce according to the directions on the jar.

8. Dish out your octopasta into two large bowls and then pour on your sauce.

9. Sprinkle the grated cheese over it and serve. Yum!

HOT BANANA BOATS

The mixture of hot banana, melted marshmallows, and gooey chocolate makes a delicious dessert.

You will need:

4 big bananas • 2 tablespoons mini marshmallows (or bigger ones torn into pieces) • 2 tablespoons chocolate chips

1. Ask an adult to preheat the oven to 375°F.

2. Hold one of the bananas so that its curved outer edge is pressed against the table.

3. Push the tip of your butter knife halfway into the curved edge of the banana.

4. Make a slit from just below the stem to just before the end of the banana.

5. Repeat this for the other bananas.

6. Stuff as many chocolate chips and mini marshmallows as you can into each banana. Any that don't fit, eat yourself!

7. Wrap each of your stuffed bananas tightly in tinfoil.

8. Ask an adult to put your bananas into the oven for ten minutes and to take them out when they are done.

9. Leave the bananas to cool for ten minutes and then unwrap and enjoy!

Warning: These bananas are extremely hot. Make sure you get an adult to check them before you start unwrapping them or you could burn your hands and mouth.

Draw your favorite summer meal.

TRAVEL GAMES

Try out these travel games to make time fly
on boring car rides.

THE PACKING GAME

Take turns adding to a list of things you pack in your suitcase. The first player starts the game by saying, "I packed my suitcase. . . ," and then chooses an item to pack in it. For example, ". . .and I put in a towel."

The next person has to add another item. So they might say, "I packed my suitcase and I put in a towel and an alarm clock."

Anyone who forgets an item while repeating the list is out.

The game continues until only one player remains.

CATEGORIES

Think of five categories of different things. For example, fruits, sports, countries, animals, and boys' names.

Now pick a letter, for instance, B. Give everyone two minutes to write down things beginning with B that match each category—the fruit might be a banana, the sport could be basketball, the country could be Brazil, the animal could be a baboon, the boy's name could be Ben, and so on.

Each player gets one point for every category they have filled and two points if they gave an answer that nobody else got. Keep playing with new rounds and new letters—the first person to reach fifty points wins the game.

TWENTY QUESTIONS

One person thinks of a famous person, place, or thing, such as Napoleon, the North Pole, or the Statue of Liberty. Then everybody else asks up to twenty questions to guess what it is. Note— the answer to the questions can only be *yes* or *no*. For example, "Are you a person?" or "Are you still alive?"

The first person to guess the answer wins, and then it's their turn to pick a person, place, or thing.

What can he see from the car window?

PICTURE PUZZLER

Tackle these picture puzzles. The first one is a brainteaser, the second one is a brain-buster! Check your answers on page 93.

Complete this grid so that the four different pictures shown below appear in every row, in every column, and in each outlined block of four squares.

Want a harder puzzle? Try completing the grid below, so the nine different pictures shown at the bottom of the page appear in every row, every column, and in each outlined block of nine squares. Good luck!

24

WORLD SPORTS CHALLENGE

Sports stars come from all over the world. This challenge puts your sports knowledge to the test. The answers are on page 93.

Can you match the star with the sport that made him famous? The first one has been done for you.

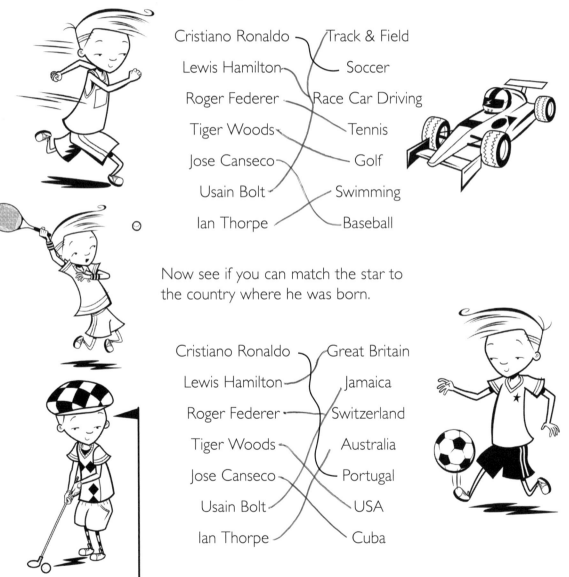

Cristiano Ronaldo — Track & Field

Lewis Hamilton — Soccer

Roger Federer — Race Car Driving

Tiger Woods — Tennis

Jose Canseco — Golf

Usain Bolt — Swimming

Ian Thorpe — Baseball

Now see if you can match the star to the country where he was born.

Cristiano Ronaldo — Great Britain

Lewis Hamilton — Jamaica

Roger Federer — Switzerland

Tiger Woods — Australia

Jose Canseco — Portugal

Usain Bolt — USA

Ian Thorpe — Cuba

POOL GAMES

Are you tired of lying by the pool? Jump in and play these superfun pool games and start having a seriously splashing time.

SHARK!

One player is the "shark" and must position himself on one side of the pool. The other players are the "fish" and must start out at the other side of the pool.

The fish must try to get to the shark's side of the pool without the shark tagging them. When all the fish have either made it to the other side or have been tagged, play the game again with any captured fish now acting as sharks. The fish that lasts the longest before being tagged is the winner.

MARCO POLO

This is a tag game named after the famous explorer Marco Polo, and it is played in the pool.

One player is "Marco" and must keep his eyes closed the whole time. The other players scatter around the pool. However, whenever Marco shouts out "Marco," all the other players must reply "Polo." Marco has to figure out where they are from their replies and try to "tag" them. The last player tagged becomes the next Marco.

PEARL DIVER

For this game you need "pearls" to throw into the pool. A pearl should be something that sinks, such as a set of keys or a small plastic bottle filled with stones. You need one less pearl than there are players or "divers."

Throw the pearls into the pool. Each diver must find a pearl. The diver who doesn't find a pearl is out. Take one pearl away and begin the game again. Continue until you have one winning diver.

Remember to take out any remaining pearls from the pool after you have finished playing.

WHAT'S DIFFERENT?

There are fifteen differences between the underwater scenes below.
Can you find them? You can check your answers on page 93.

ISLAND DISCOVERY

Test your map-reading skills by studying the map below.
Can you answer the questions using the compass above to help you?
Check your answers on page 93.

1. What number is on the sailboat to the northeast of the island? 12

2. How many round huts are located in the northwest corner of the island? 5

3. Is the giant head positioned in the east or west of the island? West

4. What tall building is at the island's southwest corner? Lighthouse

5. What is immediately east of the six palm trees? Swimming pool

6. How many flags are there on the island? 6

Now see if any of your friends and family can do it from memory. Simply let them study the map for two minutes, then cover it up and see how many questions they can answer correctly.

SUMMER SPYMASTER

Keep your secret missions secret this summer with these cool codes.

TOP SECRET MESSAGES

When you're on summer vacation and relying on postcards or e-mails to send your fellow agents instructions, it's important to be able to keep your messages top secret.

All superspies know that the best way to keep a message secret is to write it in code.

CODING MADE EASY

An easy code to use is to move each letter in your message to the next letter in the alphabet.

For example:
MEET MONDAY AT SIX

becomes:
NFFU NPOEBZ BU TJY

To make this code trickier, try getting rid of the spaces between the letters:

NFFUNPOEBZBUTJY

CODE BREAKER

A secret agent has written three messages in the code above. Can you crack the code and answer the following questions?

1. Are the files hot or cold?

2. What does he want for his dinner?

Check your answers on page 94.

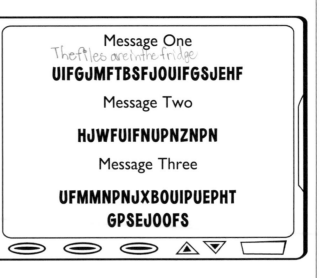

Message One

The files are in the fridge
UIFGJMFTBSFJOUIFGSJEHF

Message Two

HJWFUIFNUPNZNPN

Message Three

UFMMNPNJXBOUIPUEPHT
GPSEJOOFS

pg 30

BUILD YOUR OWN UNBREAKABLE-CODE MACHINE

Make cipher disks for you and a friend so that you can decode each other's messages. Here's how.

You will need:

a sheet of white paper • a pencil
• scissors • a blob of modeling clay
• a pen • a paper fastener
• some paper for your message

1. Place the paper over the templates at the bottom of the page.

2. Trace around both circles, using your pencil. Write the alphabet on circle A.

3. Cut out both of your circles, including the black squares on circle B.

4. Place circle B on top of circle A so that the crosses lie on top of each other. Place them on top of a lump of modeling clay and push a paper fastener through the crosses into the clay.

5. Split the fastener at the back to keep the circles together. Discard the clay.

6. To use your cipher disk, turn the top circle so that box Z shows the letter you want to write, then write the letter revealed by box 1 on your paper. For example, when A is showing in box Z, box 1 shows the letter U, so you write the letter U. Do the same for each letter of the message you want to code.

7. To use a different code, use boxes 2 or 3 instead of 1. Make sure your friend has a cipher disk and agree which box you are going to use before you send your message.

DECODING MESSAGES

To decode a message, turn the top circle so that the box you chose reveals the written letter. Then write the letter showing in box Z on your paper.

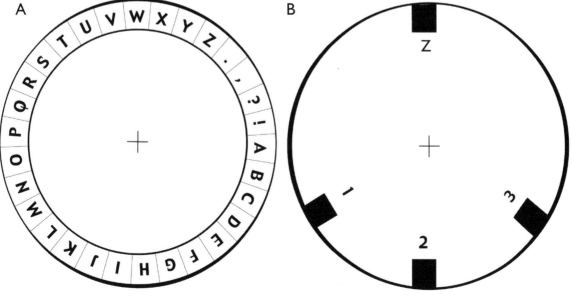

THE REAL ROBINSON CRUSOE

Four long years alone on a desert island—could you survive?

You may know the story of Robinson Crusoe—shipwrecked on an island. What you may not know is that this story is based on the adventures of a man named Alexander Selkirk.

RUNNING AWAY TO SEA

Selkirk was the son of a shoemaker and ran away from home to get rich working at sea. Selkirk went to work on a ship as a kind of pirate. The crew stole the cargo of enemy ships. It was an exciting but very dangerous job. The ship sailed in rough seas all over the world.

In 1704, Alexander Selkirk worked on a ship called the *Cinque Ports*, which sailed around the coast of South America. After a few battles and bad weather, Selkirk was convinced that the ship was in need of repair. His captain disagreed and refused to stop sailing. Selkirk demanded to be put ashore on the next island, rather than sail on a ship that he thought wasn't safe.

CAST ASHORE

The captain agreed, and Selkirk was put ashore on the island of Más a Tierra—over 372 miles off the coast of Chile in South America. He was only allowed to take a few basic tools and supplies from the ship. Selkirk decided he would wait on the island for the next passing ship to take him home.

ALL ALONE

Alone on the island, Selkirk kept a fire burning on a hill in the hope that a passing ship might see it, but none came. Months turned into years as he waited. His supplies soon ran out, but luckily there were fruits and vegetables growing on the island and goats for meat and milk. He even made clothes from the goats' skins when his own fell apart.

One day he saw two ships and rushed to the shore to meet them. But the ships belonged to the king's enemies and he had to hide. He didn't speak to or see another human for four years.

ON THE HORIZON

In 1709, he spotted a sail and an English flag. A ship! Selkirk looked like a wild man, with a long beard and wearing animal skins. Amazingly, one of the ship's crewmen recognized him from the *Cinque Ports* and he was taken aboard.

When he returned home, Selkirk met a writer who wrote of his adventures for a magazine. Later, another writer used Selkirk's story for a book, calling the hero not Alexander Selkirk . . . but Robinson Crusoe!

ISLAND ADVENTURES

Can you survive on this tropical island? Check your answers on page 94.

CROP CONUNDRUM

On your desert island you need food to eat, so you decide to grow some coconuts, bananas, and mangoes. You divide up the island into plots. Each plot of fruit can only share borders with plots of different fruit.

Can you write in the name of the right crop in each empty plot and work out what crop you are going to have in the plots marked A and B?

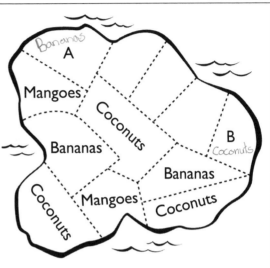

ISLAND ATTACK!

Connect the dots to see what is chasing the castaway.

33

Doodle your own awesome invention.

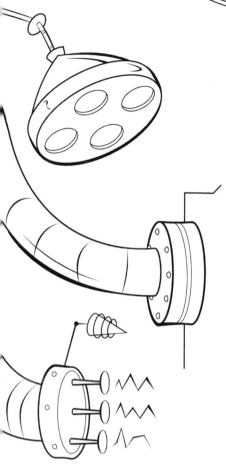

CROSSED WIRES

The inventor has tangled the cables to his inventions. Can you figure out which plug belongs to each invention? Check your answers on page 94.

Chocotoaster =

Instajellymatic =

Robobutler =

WHAT SHOULD WE DO TODAY?

Get outside and have fun with these exciting outdoor activities.

SET UP AN OBSTACLE COURSE

Set up the obstacle course below on the beach or on some grass.

Stick 3: Say the alphabet backward while rubbing your tummy and patting your head at the same time.

Stick 4: Throw a ball in the air and catch it while hopping on one leg.

Stick 4

Stick 3

Stick 2

Stick 1

Start/
Finish

Place a stick in the ground and mark a Start/Finish line.

Then place another stick roughly twelve feet away from the first and three smaller sticks spaced evenly between the two.

All competitors must complete the following tasks at each stick:

Stick 1: Take off one shoe and do ten jumping jacks on the spot.

Stick 2: Drop to the ground and do five push-ups.

Now sprint back toward the Start/Finish line. Don't forget to stop and put your shoe back on before you cross the line.

Time how long each competitor takes to complete the course using the second hand on a watch. The fastest one to cross the finish line wins.

GO CRABBING

If you are near a harbor or river, why not go crab fishing?

You will need:

a ball of string • a stick (roughly two feet long) • a net • a fishhook and small weight (from a local fishing shop) • a bucket • bacon pieces or scraps of fish from the bait shop

1. Head down to your crab fishing location with the equipment above and an adult to share the fun with. Ask people nearby to recommend a good spot.

2. Tie one end of the string to your stick—the string needs to be long enough to reach from your stick to the bottom of the water.

3. Tie the weight onto the string near the end of your line. Tie the hook securely to the end of the string. Push the bait onto the hook.

4. Drop the baited line into the water and wait for a crab to take the bait— you will feel a firm tug on your string when you've got one.

5. Slowly lift your line out of the water and catch the crab in the net. Gently transfer your crab into your bucket filled with water.

Warning: Crabs are living creatures, so treat them gently, and always put your crabs back where you caught them. Never keep crabs out of the water for longer than a couple of hours. Never go crabbing without an adult.

Design the ultimate go-kart track for the drivers to race on.

START
—
FINISH

GO-KART GRAND PRIX

Below is a picture of the ultimate go-kart.

Using the squares in the grid below to help you, can you draw it?

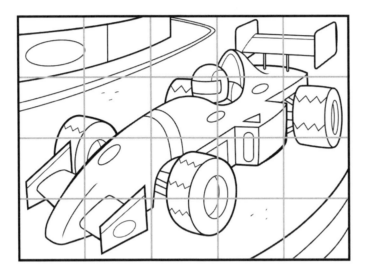

CREATE YOUR OWN SUMMER COMIC STRIP

Learn how to draw Doodles the Dog, and then make him the star of your own comic capers.

To draw Doodles, simply follow the instructions below. Practice drawing him on scrap paper before starring him in the comic strips on the next page.

You will need:

scrap paper • a pencil
• a permanent black pen
• an eraser • felt-tip pens

1. Use a pencil to draw the basic shape by drawing circles to show his head and body.

2. Draw more shapes for his nose and tail, and add his legs.

3. Use your black pen to draw the outline around the shapes. Leave areas blank where the different parts attach to his body.

4. Add Doodles's eyes and the insides of his ears.

5. Let your picture dry, then erase all of your pencil lines using your eraser. Use your felt pens to color him in.

Now you have your finished Doodles. Use him to create some crazy comic strips on the opposite page. What adventures will he have this summer?

THE ADVENTURES OF DOODLES

YOUR COMIC STRIPS!

BE A STONE-SKIPPING CHAMP

Hold a stone-skipping competition down at the water's edge—the first person to skip a stone that "bounces" six times before going "plop" wins.

HOW TO SKIP A STONE

1. Choose your stone well. A round, smooth, flat one that is roughly the size of your palm and weighs about the same as an apple is best.

2. Find an area of calm water to practice your stone-skipping technique.

3. Stand perpendicular to the water, and crouch with your feet apart.

5. Sweep your arm back, then jerk it forward. Use your wrist and index finger to spin the stone as it leaves your hand.

4. Curl your index finger around the edge of the stone and place your thumb flat on top of it. Your middle finger should be flat underneath to make sure the stone stays completely horizontal when you throw it.

Tip: The angle at which you throw the stone is very important. If the stone hits the water at an angle that is too steep, its edge will catch and it will sink. If the angle is too shallow, the stone will glide along without bouncing. Practice until you achieve a perfect skipper.

MESSAGE IN A BOTTLE

You are strolling by the sea skipping stones when all of a sudden
you spy a bottle. Then another, and then another.
You notice that each bottle contains a rolled up piece of paper . . .

1. On the paper inside the first bottle,
you find the following cryptic message:

**"X L M T I Z G F O Z G R L M H!
B L F   S Z E V   D L M   Z   U I V V
R X V   X I V Z N!"**

Need a clue to decode it? Write the
alphabet backward under a normal
alphabet and substitute each letter in
the message for the letter below it.
Can you figure out what it says?

2. You look inside the second bottle
and find this message:

K I V H V M G   G S V H V

**N V H H Z T V H   Z G   Q L V' H
X Z U V   G L   X O Z R N . . .**

Can you figure out what it means?

3. The third bottle contains an even
stranger-looking message. On the
paper you find the grid below and this
cryptic message:

**"Color in the squares you need,
to show you something you can read."**

Can you crack the code?

All the answers are on page 94.

2 4 7	A	E	G	E	L	A	R
1 3 6 7	A	S	G	S	O	A	L
2 5	F	K	H	O	E	M	E
1 3 6	F	M	L	A	D	B	E
1 4 5	M	L	E	U	A	M	O
2 3 5 6 7	N	E	F	A	W	M	L
1 3 4 6 7	A	D	A	A	E	A	H

GONE CAMPING

Have fun at the campsite with these cool camping activities and puzzles.

BUILD A BASE CAMP

Why not make use of all the trees around you and create your very own camouflaged base camp?

You will need:

a ball of string • scissors • a large bedsheet or tarp • 3 sturdy sticks roughly 5 feet long • 1 stick roughly 6.5 feet long

1. Find a tree with a forked branch.

2. Take the three shorter sticks and tie them together with some string to form a tripod shape. Push the sticks into the ground at a forty-five degree angle.

3. Place the longer stick on top of the

Rest the other end of the stick in the fork of the tree, as shown above.

4. Carefully lay the sheet over the frame. Secure it by placing heavy stones on the ends of the sheet so that it doesn't blow away.

5. Cover your tent with wet leaves or mud to camouflage it.

TENT TROUBLE

To solve this puzzle you must add tents into the boxes on the grid, so that every tree has at least one tent horizontally or vertically next to it (but not diagonally).

Beside each row and below each column is a number that tells you how many tents they contain.

No tent can be in a square that is right next to another tent (not even diagonally).

When every tree has a tent, and all the numbers are correct, you've cracked the tent teaser.

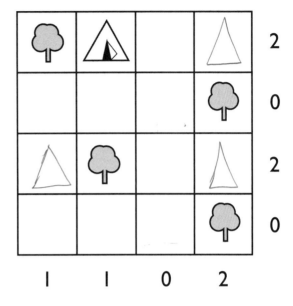

Now try finding the tents in the larger grid below—this one is a bit harder, but it works in exactly the same way. We've started you off with the first tent. Can you find where the missing tents are?

Check your answers on page 94.

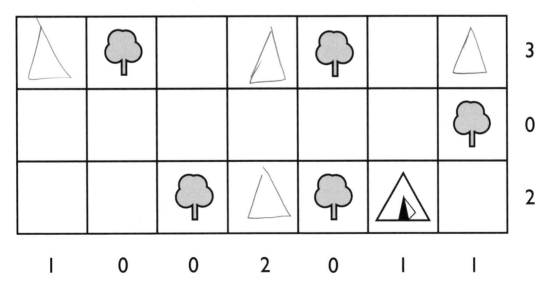

45

ROLLER-COASTER RIDE

Everybody loves going to the theme park.

If you can't ride a real roller coaster, have fun cracking these roller-coaster-themed puzzles instead—you'll find all the answers on page 94.

STAR SPOTTING

Can you find twenty stars hidden in this picture?

DID YOU KNOW?

Over five hundred years ago, the Russians invented a slide that you could ride on— very much like a roller coaster. The structure came to be known as the Russian Ice Slides because riders climbed up wooden stairs attached to a large slide that was covered in ice. They then slid down the slope of ice and were propelled up to the top of another slide. By the 1780s, millions of people had flocked to try these sliding rides. It is believed these slides became the model for the modern roller coaster that you can see today.

COASTER CONUNDRUM

These four circles represent roller coasters that loop, twist, go upside down, and go backward.

Where the circles overlap, the coasters do more than one thing. For example, area *J* is for coasters that twist and go upside down and area *D* is for coasters that go backward and loop.

Can you figure out what area is for coasters that twist, loop, and go upside down, but do not go backward?

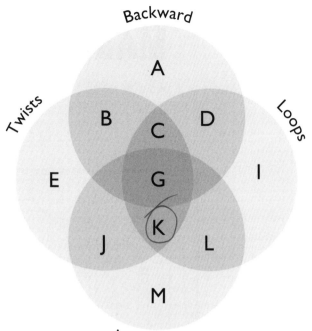

RON'S ON

Roller-Coaster Ron loves to ride.

He doesn't wear headphones while riding.

He never wears zippers or buttons.

Can you spot him?

47

MASTER BUILDER

Below is a picture of the Taj Mahal, a beautiful building in India.
Every year, millions of tourists flock to admire it.

Using the squares in the grid below to help you, can you draw it?

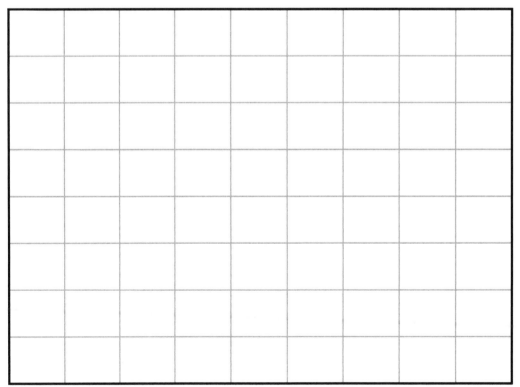

HIT THE BEACH

The beach is always lots of fun. There are twenty shells in this picture. Can you find them all? Check your answer on page 95.

SOGGY SUMMER GAMES

Even the sunniest summers have a rainy day or two. Here are some great games to keep you busy until the sun comes out.

DON'T LOSE YOUR MARBLES

You will need:

two to six players • a long piece of string • 13 small marbles •1 big marble for each player to use as a Shooter

1. Use your string to form the outline of a circle on the floor roughly three feet across. This is your marble arena.

2. Place the thirteen small marbles in the center of the circle. It's up to you how you position them—you could arrange them in a cluster or even have them scattered randomly around the circle.

3. The youngest player goes first. Kneel at any point outside the circle and lean inward so that the hand that is holding the Shooter is inside the circle.

4. To shoot your marble, place your knuckles on the floor, with the Shooter

held in your curled index finger.

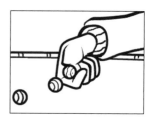

5. Use your thumb to flick the Shooter at a smaller marble in the circle.

The aim is to knock these marbles out of the circle, while keeping the Shooter inside the circle. Each marble that is knocked out is worth one point. If your Shooter stays inside the circle, you get to shoot again starting from where it lands.

6. Your turn ends when you either fail to knock out any marbles or the Shooter ends up outside the circle. It is then the turn of the player to your left.

7. Keep playing until all the marbles have been knocked out of the circle. The player with the most points wins.

CRAZY CARD-TOSS CAPERS

You will need:

at least two players

• a pack of cards • a hat or large bowl

TOP TECHNIQUE

1. To hold the card, place one of the corners between your index finger and your middle finger with your knuckles bent. Rotate your hand at the wrist, bringing the card toward you, and then flick it forward, at the same time releasing your grip on the card. Try to flick your wrist sharply outward so that your card flies forward and away from you.

2. Practice shooting your cards at different targets around the room, and when you think you have mastered the skill, it is time to play.

3. Place the hat or bowl on the floor. Players should sit or stand roughly nine feet away from it.

4. Divide a pack of cards evenly among the number of players.

5. Each player takes turns trying to flick one of his cards into the hat. If the card goes in, he gets another turn. Otherwise play passes to the next player. Keep score as you go.

6. The winner of each round is the player who gets the most cards into the hat. The first player to win five rounds is the card-toss champion.

SUMMER AT THE CIRCUS

Step right up! The circus has come to town.
Tackle the puzzles and check your answers on page 95.

PUT UP THE BIG TOP

Can you figure out which of the boxes
contains all of the right pieces to build
this circus tent?

A

B

C

D

THE HUMAN CANNONBALL

Last time Harry was fired from the cannon, he landed nine feet beyond and
six feet to the left of the net. For his next attempt, should he move the
cannon nine feet further away and six feet to the right, or nine feet toward
the net and six feet to the left?

FIND THE SQUARES

All of the squares below can be found in the picture of this superstrong man.

Can you find out where each square belongs? Write down the letter of the column and the number of the row in which it appears.

Tip: The squares aren't necessarily the right way up.

CLOWNING AROUND

This juggling clown has lots of balls in the air.

There are seven pairs of balls that are exactly the same and only one ball that is unique.

Can you find the ball that doesn't have a match?

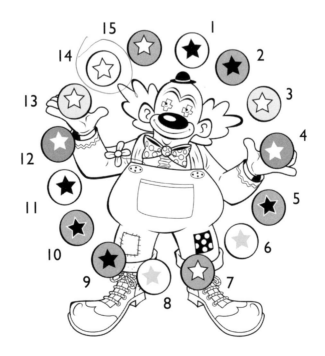

CIRCUS SKILLS

Summer vacation is the perfect time to master the art of juggling so you can wow your friends.

JUGGLING BASICS

1. Begin with one ball. Stand with your arms bent and your hands shoulder-width apart. Throw the ball from one hand to the other and back. Make sure that the ball reaches the height of your eyes with every throw. Keep throwing one ball until you manage to throw it and catch it the same way every time without thinking.

2. Now add another ball. Hold one ball in each hand. Throw the first ball up as you did in step 1. When the first ball reaches eye height and is just about to come down, throw the second ball. This will leave your hand empty just in time to catch the first ball. This is called the "exchange." Practice this over and over again until you get into a rhythm.

3. Now you are ready to try three balls. Hold two balls in one hand and one in the other. The action is exactly the same as the exchange you practiced in step 2 with two balls. Throw the first ball, then throw the second ball just before you catch the first. This time you need to throw the third ball just before you catch the second. This is called a "pass."

4. To begin with, doing one pass will be quite difficult. But try to increase the number of passes each time you practice to become an expert juggler. Once you've managed three passes in a row, you are juggling!

Tip: Keep your eyes straight ahead, looking at the top of your throws.

A BAG OF TRICKS

When you're comfortable with three balls, you can try some tricks.

TRICK ONE: Cool Crossover

Start with two balls in one hand and one in the other. Throw the first ball (from the hand with two balls) straight up, a little higher than normal. Then throw the other two at the same time so they cross over above your head. Catch the first ball with the hand you threw it from and then continue to juggle as normal.

TRICK TWO: One-Hand Wonder

Hold two balls in one hand. Throw the first ball straight up. Move your hand to the right and throw the second ball up before quickly moving your hand back to catch the first. Catch the first and throw it again as you move to catch the second. The balls should be going straight up and down while your hand moves from side to side.

THE GOLDEN RULE

Once you've learned how to juggle, you will never forget how to do it. The key to improvement is practice.

HANDS UP FOR HANJIE

Try out this game and time will fly . . .

Hanjie is a great Japanese drawing puzzle in which you use numbers to figure out which squares in a grid to shade. As you shade in more and more squares, the picture reveals itself.

The numbers tell you how many squares to shade in a particular row or column. For example, the numbers *3, 3* at the side of a row tell you that you need to shade in a group of three squares together and then leave a gap of at least one square before shading in another group of three squares somewhere in that row.

HOW TO HANJIE

Take a look at the puzzle below to see how it's done, and then try the Hanjie puzzle on the opposite page.

1. Since the grid is five squares across, you know that any row with a 5 next to it is all shaded in.

2. Fill in the columns that have *3,1,4* above them. Each of these columns is ten squares long so you can be sure that if you shade 3, 1, and then 4 squares together leaving a gap between each block, you have used up the column.

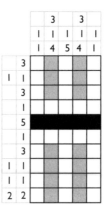

3. Then there are three rows with just a 3 by them, so we can complete three groups of three.

4. Finally, complete the 5 in the middle column and the two 2s in the bottom row to finish your Hanjie.

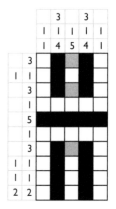

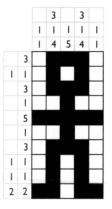

56

HIGH-FLYING HANJIE

Try this Hanjie puzzle. Some squares have been done for you.
Check your answers on page 95.

Tip: If a Hanjie puzzle is ten squares wide (like this one) and a column
or row has the number *10* by it, you can shade in all ten squares in that row
or column.

Sometimes you will know that a square is definitely NOT shaded. In that case,
put a little dot in it to remind you. It will help you out later!

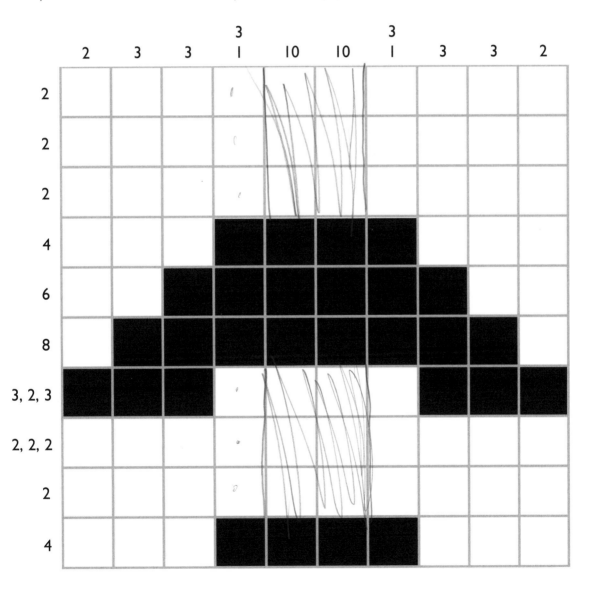

ULTIMATE I-SPY

Keep your eyes peeled to make long car rides more fun.

You can play this game with as many people as you'd like. When each item on the list below is spotted, write the initials of the person who found it first in the box.

When all the items have been spotted, the person who found the most items wins.

1. A yellow car		15. A tent	
2. A mailbox		16. A horse trailer	
3. A tree with no leaves		17. A traffic jam	
4. A river		18. A sports car	
5. A traffic light		19. Someone running	
6. A water tower		20. A sign for a theme park	
7. A red truck		21. A gas station	
8. A worm		22. A hot-air balloon	
9. A cow		23. Graffiti	
10. A church		24. A child on roller skates	
11. A castle		25. A woman in a purple hat	
12. A flag		26. A police car	
13. A bird of prey		27. A broken-down vehicle	
14. A tractor		28. A bridge	

WHAT WILL YOU BE?

A movie star? A soccer player? A president? An astronaut? Take this quiz.
Then turn the page to find out what your answers say about your future!

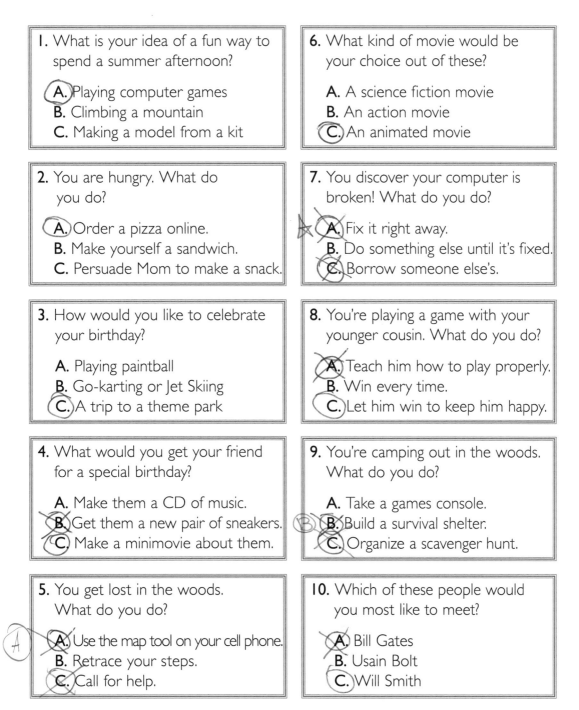

1. What is your idea of a fun way to spend a summer afternoon?

   A. Playing computer games
   B. Climbing a mountain
   C. Making a model from a kit

2. You are hungry. What do you do?

   A. Order a pizza online.
   B. Make yourself a sandwich.
   C. Persuade Mom to make a snack.

3. How would you like to celebrate your birthday?

   A. Playing paintball
   B. Go-karting or Jet Skiing
   C. A trip to a theme park

4. What would you get your friend for a special birthday?

   A. Make them a CD of music.
   B. Get them a new pair of sneakers.
   C. Make a minimovie about them.

5. You get lost in the woods. What do you do?

   A. Use the map tool on your cell phone.
   B. Retrace your steps.
   C. Call for help.

6. What kind of movie would be your choice out of these?

   A. A science fiction movie
   B. An action movie
   C. An animated movie

7. You discover your computer is broken! What do you do?

   A. Fix it right away.
   B. Do something else until it's fixed.
   C. Borrow someone else's.

8. You're playing a game with your younger cousin. What do you do?

   A. Teach him how to play properly.
   B. Win every time.
   C. Let him win to keep him happy.

9. You're camping out in the woods. What do you do?

   A. Take a games console.
   B. Build a survival shelter.
   C. Organize a scavenger hunt.

10. Which of these people would you most like to meet?

   A. Bill Gates
   B. Usain Bolt
   C. Will Smith

WHAT YOUR ANSWERS MEAN

Count up how many times you have answered A, B, or C in the quiz on page 59. Read on to reveal what your answers say about your future.

Mostly As

You are a techno whiz.

You love technology and are good at using it. If humans ever get to Mars, you'll be on the first spacecraft to land. You would make a great scientist, doctor, computer game designer, or even an astronaut. Your brilliant mind could lead to you inventing cool things that could make you a very rich man!

Mostly Bs

You are an action hero.

Brave and adventurous, you could be an explorer, soldier, or film stuntman. You like to win, which could help you take your chosen sport to the highest level—a World Cup maybe, or the Olympic Games. Your practical mind could help you to lead expeditions to faraway places.

Mostly Cs

You are a creative genius.

Artistic and fun to be around, you could be an actor, director, or musician. You like talking to people and making them feel good, so people like to be around you. You're comfortable in the spotlight and are looking forward to people lining up for your latest film, your new album, or just for your autograph!

WACKY SUMMER SPORTS

Read on to find out about some weird and wacky sports you could get into this summer.

BELGIUM: Bathtub Sailing

Is it a sailboat? Is it a canoe? No . . . it is the International Regatta of Bathtubs. Held in the town of Dinant in August, hopefuls in fancy clothes race their bathtubs down the River Meuse, hoping to reach the finish line first.

Pelting spectators and other competitors with buckets of water is encouraged, but using any kind of engine is strictly forbidden.

USA: Hot-Dog Eating

Every Fourth of July at a restaurant on Coney Island in New York, people from all over the world come to watch twenty competitors compete in the annual hot-dog eating contest. Contestants must eat as many hot dogs and buns as they can in just twelve minutes. Winning contestants often manage to stuff their faces with more than fifty hot dogs in that time.

Warning: This sort of extreme eating takes lots of training, and should not be attempted at home.

ENGLAND: Cheese Rolling

At the end of May, in a small town in Gloucestershire, a group of brave people gather to chase a large, round cheese down a very steep hill. During the event, the enormous cheese can reach speeds of seventy miles per hour. Competitors have been known to break bones in this cheesy quest.

WALES: Bog Snorkeling

Every August, a small village in Wales hosts the International Bog-Snorkeling Championships. People come from all over the world to swim two lengths through the thick, brown water as fast as they can wearing flippers and snorkels. One competitor from Australia described her experience as like "swimming through pea soup." Yuck!

WORLD RALLY

Start your engines. It's time to race!

Each player must place a coin on the starting line. Take turns spinning the spinner to move your coin. You must follow the instructions on the square that you land on. The first person to complete three laps wins.

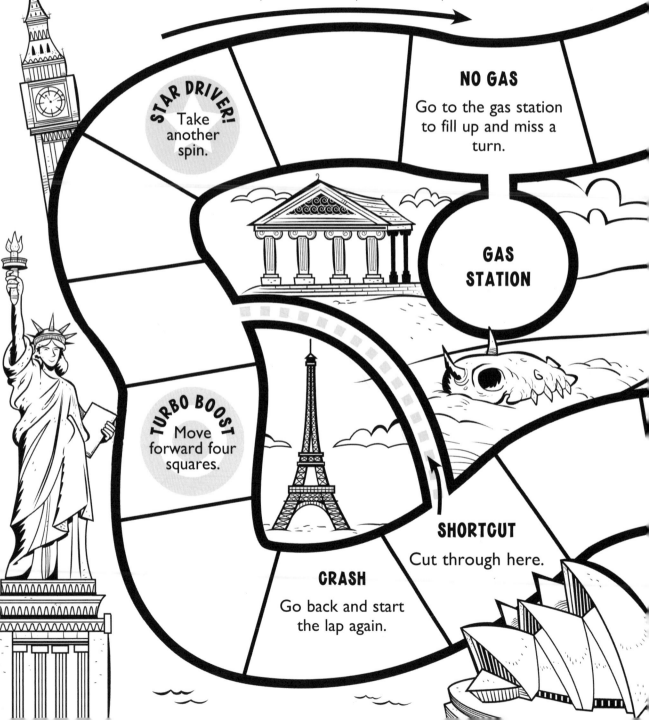

STAR DRIVER! Take another spin.

NO GAS
Go to the gas station to fill up and miss a turn.

GAS STATION

TURBO BOOST Move forward four squares.

SHORTCUT
Cut through here.

CRASH
Go back and start the lap again.

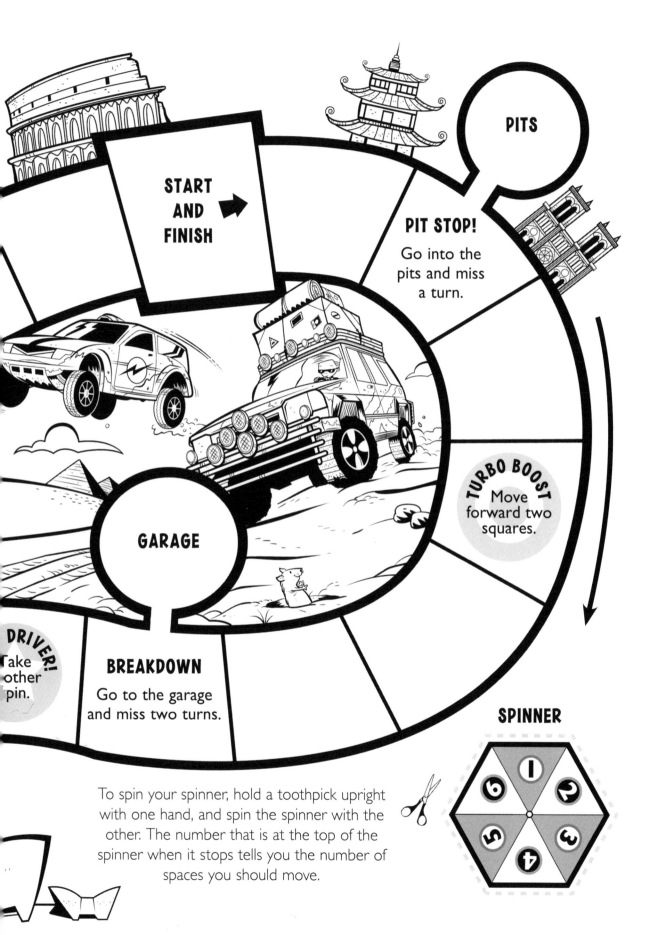

PITS

**START
AND
FINISH** ➡️

PIT STOP!
Go into the
pits and miss
a turn.

TURBO BOOST
Move
forward two
squares.

GARAGE

DRIVER!
Take
other
pin.

BREAKDOWN
Go to the garage
and miss two turns.

SPINNER

To spin your spinner, hold a toothpick upright
with one hand, and spin the spinner with the
other. The number that is at the top of the
spinner when it stops tells you the number of
spaces you should move.

Complete the battle on board!

BACK OF SPINNER

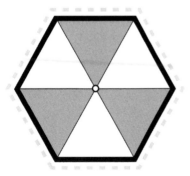

THE LEGEND OF BLACKBEARD

Of all the pirates who ever lived, perhaps the most feared was "Blackbeard."
Read all about his pirating misadventures below.

Captain Blackbeard was born in Bristol, England, around 1680. His real name remains uncertain—either Edward Drummond or Edward Teach, no one is sure. When he grew up, he left Bristol and headed for the island of Jamaica in the Caribbean. There he joined the crew of Benjamin Hornigold, a pirate captain, who taught him how to ambush ships and steal their cargo.

Together, they ambushed a ship and took it for themselves. Arming it with forty cannons, they named it *The Queen Anne's Revenge*. Blackbeard soon became captain of this ship, with his own fearsome crew.

Blackbeard got his name because before an attack he would tie his beard together with black ribbons. He then stuffed rope under his pirate hat and set it on fire, making him look very scary, indeed!

His most famous mission was a raid on a port on the East Coast of America in 1718. Blackbeard stole the cargo of five ships, taking several people hostage in the process. He escaped with a mighty stash of booty, but not before releasing the hostages unharmed—and without their clothes!

Blackbeard hoped to retire rich after this raid, but two American captains named Maynard and Hyde had other ideas. They both went off in pursuit of the troublesome pirate.

They finally found him on the morning of November 22, 1718. A bloody battle took place, with Hyde and six of his men killed in an attack from Blackbeard's cannons.

Blackbeard died that day from pistol and sword wounds. Maynard sailed away from the bloody scene triumphant, with the pirate captain's head hanging from the bow of his ship.

MAKE YOUR OWN TREASURE MAP

Beaches are great places for burying stuff as any good pirate knows, and a pirate who wants to stash his booty needs to make a map so he can find it again.

BURY YOUR TREASURE

Bury your treasure—a candy bar that's completely sealed to keep out the sand is perfect.

Mark the spot with a stick until you have made your map.

WHICH WAY IS NORTH?

First you need to figure out which way is north. To do this, move your body so you are facing the sun. In the morning the sun is in the east, and in the afternoon the sun is in the west.

Stretch your arms out to your sides and turn your body so that your left arm is pointing west and your right arm is pointing east. The direction your nose is pointing in is north.

Choose an object that won't move, such as a tree. Starting at the tree, walk toward your treasure, counting your paces (make sure your steps are all roughly the same size). If you have to change direction to avoid something, write down the number of paces you have taken, write down the new direction you have to walk in, and start counting from one again.

MAP-MAKING

On a piece of paper, mark your treasure with an X and mark the tree. Draw a line from the treasure to the tree.

Now write out the directions from the tree. For example:

From the tree, take twelve paces north, five paces east, three paces north, six paces west, and ten paces south. X marks the spot where my treasure is buried!

Remove the stick that marks your treasure and smooth the sand over it so the treasure is well hidden.

Hand the map to your friends and see if they can find your buried treasure.

TREASURE HUNT

Blackbeard's treasure map has been found!

He has buried two swords, two amulets, two keys, and two bars of Spanish silver. Their locations are shown in this grid map. But he forgot to mark where the swords are and where he has hidden the missing key. Can you find them in the grid map below? See if you have located them correctly on page 95.

HOW TO PLAY

1. The numbers beside each row and under each column tell you how many squares in that row or that column are occupied. For example, the top row has the numbers *1* and *2* by it, which tells you that three squares are occupied— one square on its own and then two squares right next to each other.

2. You can see where the two amulets are, both bars of silver, and one of the keys that have been buried. Can you work out where the two swords and the missing key are hidden?

Tip: Start by putting an *X* in squares that you know are occupied, and an *O* in squares you know are empty. When you have an *X* or an *O* in each of the squares, you should be able to figure out what lies buried beneath them.

THE TREASURE

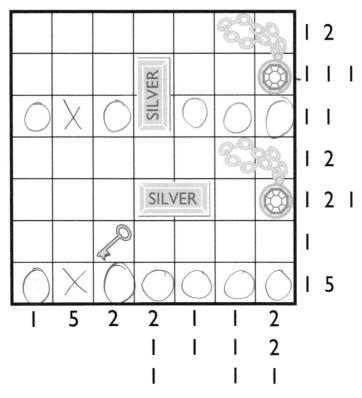

AMULET   SWORD

SILVER   KEY

THE GRID MAP

67

WHIRLYBIRD HELICOPTERS

Whirlybirds are paper helicopters—throw them up in the air or drop them from up high and they'll twirl downward slowly like helicopters coming in to land. They're easy to make, fun to decorate, and great to play with.

Follow the instructions on the opposite page to make your whirlybird.

To throw your whirlybird, hold it by the paper clip and toss it in the air—if you have made it correctly, it should spin all the way back to the ground.

A simple game to play with a friend is to throw your whirlybirds up in the air at the same time. The one that hits the ground last wins.

Alternatively, you could play the Target Game.

TARGET GAME

You need to make a "target" by drawing two circles, one inside the other, on a piece of paper. To do this, place a dinner plate on a piece of paper and draw around it. Place a smaller plate in the center and draw around it to form an inner circle. Cut around the outer circle. Now place your target on the ground.

You can play this game with as many people as you want. Players throw their whirlybirds up in the air at the same time and see whose lands closest to the center of the target. Score one point if your whirlybird lands touching the outer circle and three points if it lands touching the inner circle. The player with the most points after six rounds wins the game.

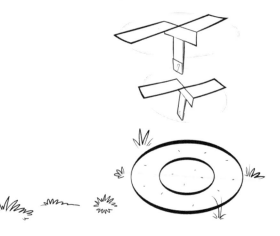

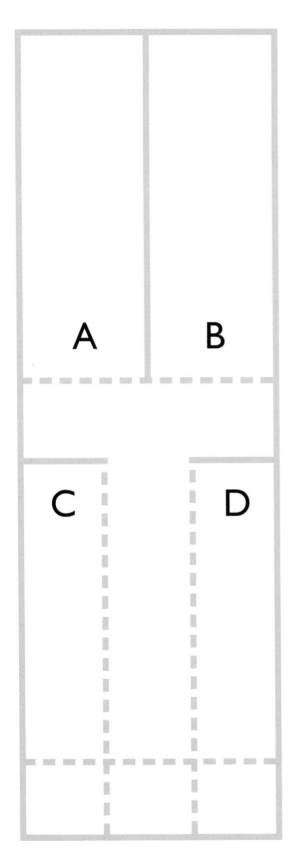

MAKING A WHIRLYBIRD

You will need:

a sheet of paper • markers
• paper clips • a pair of scissors

1. Draw the pattern opposite onto the sheet of paper and cut it out. Decorate it using markers (or crayons) to make your whirlybird stand out from the crowd.

2. Using scissors, carefully cut along the solid lines of the pattern.

3. Fold section A forward and fold section B back so that they now are suspended at a ninety-degree angle to the rest of the paper.

4. Fold along the dotted lines of pieces C and D, folding one forward and one back. Press them together to make a three-layered sandwich in the middle.

5. Fold the flap up from the bottom—it doesn't matter which way—and secure with a paper clip. This will add a little weight to the bottom of the whirlybird that will help it fall to the ground more easily.

Tip:
Add extra paperclips to the flap at the bottom of your whirlybird to make it spin to the ground faster.

ROAD TRIP

Have you ever imagined taking a road trip in the car of your dreams?
If so, you'll enjoy being behind the wheel on this puzzle adventure.

TRAVEL ADVENTURE

You've decided to take a road trip across America. You're going to take three
separate car rides, and one airplane flight. Can you work out which cities you will
pass through on each trip described below? Write down which three cities you
will not visit because you don't pass through the squares in which they appear.
The answers are on page 95.

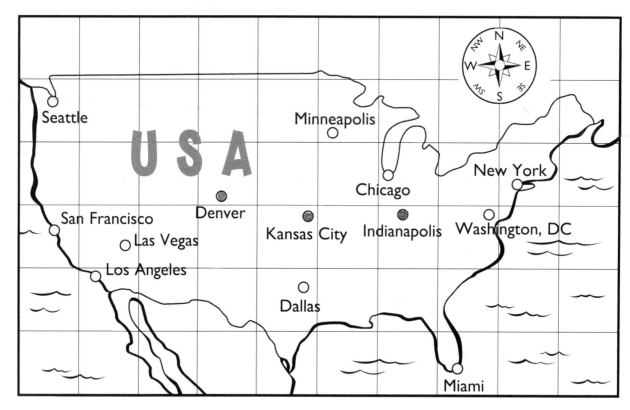

Trip A: From New York, you drive
one square west, then three squares
south, then one square north, then six
squares west. Los Angeles

Trip B: You fly to Seattle. From there
you drive five squares east, then one

square south, then one square east, then
five squares west, then one square south.
Las Vegas

Trip C: From Las Vegas, you drive one
square south, then six squares east, then
two squares north and one square east.
New York

Design the car you would drive on a road trip.

PUZZLE CITY

The city never sleeps and neither will you with these puzzles keeping you awake. All the answers are on page 95.

CAPITAL CITY CHECKLIST

Match the capital cities to the countries in which they are found. The first one has been done for you.

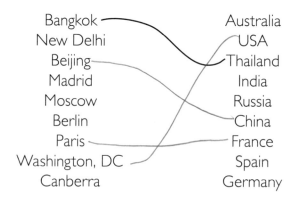

Bangkok   Australia
New Delhi   USA
Beijing   Thailand
Madrid   India
Moscow   Russia
Berlin   China
Paris   France
Washington, DC   Spain
Canberra   Germany

AROUND THE BLOCK

Follow the directions below and see where you would end up.

Turn right out of garage A and take the first right. Turn right again, then take the first left. Take the second right, then turn left and then take the first left.

Which garage do you end up in, B or C?

Garage C

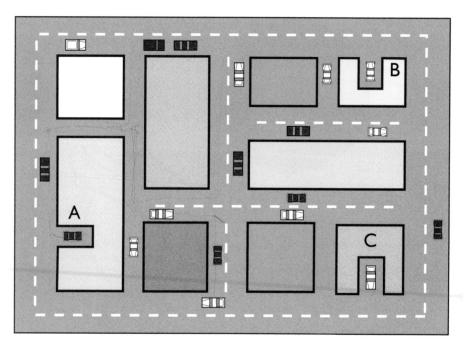

RAINY DAY GAMES

If it's too wet to play outside, why not try these finger-flicking indoor ball games?

TABLE-TOP FOOTBALL

1. Find three coins, a table, and someone to play with.

2. Sit opposite each other. Player *A* makes a goal by placing his fist against the edge of the table, with his first and fourth fingers stretched out on top.

3. Player *B* positions the three coins in a triangle—one coin behind the other two. He then flicks the back coin with his finger, attempting to shoot it between the front two coins and into the goal.

4. If Player *B* scores a goal, fails to shoot his coin between the front two coins, or if he blasts his coin off the table, it is Player *A*'s turn to shoot.

First to score five goals wins the game.

INDOOR CRAZY GOLF

1. Find some paper, empty toilet paper rolls, a few books, and someone to play with.

2. Scrunch up nine balls of paper tightly—these will be your "hole balls." Place the "hole balls" on the floor around the room, and position the empty toilet paper rolls and books between them.

3. Make a "golf ball" by scrunching up another sheet of paper.

4. Take turns flicking the "golf ball" so that it passes around or through the obstacles and hits each of the "hole balls."

Record how many flicks it takes each player to hit each "hole ball" on the course. The player who completes the course in the lowest number of flicks wins.

CARS, PLANES, AND TRAINS

Kick-start your brain into gear with these perplexing puzzles.
Check your answers on page 95.

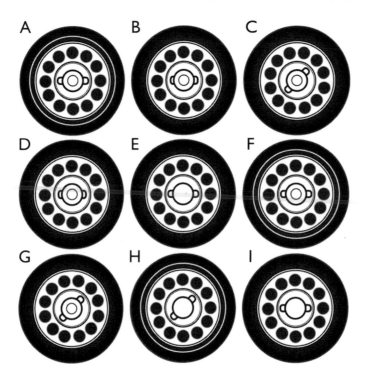

WHICH WHEELS?

These nine wheels look very similar, but in fact there are four matching pairs and one wheel which is not like any other.

Can you pick out the four pairs and spot the wheel that doesn't belong?

Wheel H

BITS 'N' PIECES

Only one of the boxes below contains all the shapes needed to make this picture of a plane.

Can you figure out which box it is?

TRAIN TRACKER

The three squares below all appear in the main picture of the train. See if you can find them all. Once you have found each square, write down its coordinates—this is the exact location of the square in the grid. To write down the coordinates of a square, simply write down the letter of the row and the number of the column in which it appears.

DOWN ON THE FARM

Put on your boots and prepare to get dirty down on the farm.
See page 96 for the answers.

ANIMALS EVERYWHERE

If you visit a farm, you'll find creatures you rarely see in the city.
There are twenty animals and birds in this picture—can you find them all?

CONNECT THE DOTS

Connect the dots in the correct order to find out what this boy is feeding.

FIELD WORK

Farmer Brown has four sheep and four pigs in his field.

Can you draw two straight lines across the field to divide it into four areas? Each area must have one sheep and one pig in it.

SPOOKY STORY

Sitting around a campfire sharing spooky stories is tons of fun.
Here are some storytelling tips, and a story to give everyone the creeps.

STORYTELLING TIPS

1. Point a flashlight under your chin shining upward to make your face look eerie.

2. Pretend the tale you are about to tell is a true story and that you read it in a magazine somewhere...

3. Keep your voice quiet so everyone has to lean forward to hear you.

4. When you get to the scary ending, leave a long pause before you deliver it. Say the last words much LOUDER.

A TRUE STORY

Grandpa Henry had been dead for a couple of years, and his grandson, Ben, missed him very much. Grandpa was buried in the cemetery next to Ben's house, and Ben could see the grave from his bedroom window.

One night, Ben dreamed he woke to find himself alone in the house. His parents were nowhere to be found. A storm raged outside. The wind howled, and broken branches crashed across the garden.

Suddenly the phone rang. Ben picked it up... it was the voice of Grandpa!

"Don't be scared Ben, you're having a dream. You will wake up soon," said Grandpa's voice.

Ben woke up. He peered out of his window and saw that there had in fact been a real storm and the grass was strewed with fallen branches. He saw that the telephone line to the house had broken and the wire hung down right over Grandpa Henry's grave ...

Ben turned from the window, thinking what a strange coincidence it was. At that moment, he heard a noise... it was the noise of the PHONE RINGING!

BUILD A
SAND CASTLE FORT

To make the most impressive sand castle on the beach,
follow the tips below.

1. Choose an area close enough to the sea so you don't have to walk miles to get water. Draw a big square with a stick, and pour water over it to make the sand firm.

2. Pile a mound of sand on top of the square area. Pour water all over it and pat it firmly down with your shovel. This will give you a solid base to build your castle on.

3. Fill a bucket with sand, pat the sand in firmly, then turn the bucket over to produce the main body of a tower.

4. To make the turret on top, shape a thick disk of wet sand and gently flatten it with the palm of your hand. Place a smaller disk on top, and another smaller disk on top, making a cone shape. Smooth out the sides of your turret.

5. Make four towers, as shown below, and connect them with strong walls of damp sand. Make the walls thicker at the bottom so they won't fall over.

6. Make a door in your walls by gently tunneling in at the bottom, scraping out sand gradually with your finger until you have carved an arched entrance.

7. Dig a moat around the base of your castle. Leave a bridge across it to the door and wait for the water to come in and fill up the moat.

Tip: Using your finger, carve the outline of bricks on your castle walls.

SUMMER FUN ON MAIN STREET

Have fun in town with these super puzzles.
Check your answers on page 96.

WHERE TO MEET?

You are meeting a friend on Main Street, but you've forgotten where! You remember it wasn't at either end of the street, and it wasn't at a store that began with B. It wasn't next door to the hair salon or opposite the bookstore, so where were you supposed to meet?

You meet your friend, then cross the street and spend ten minutes in the store opposite. Then you turn left out of that store and go three stores along and stop in that store. Then you cross the street again to the store opposite. Did you buy a book, a belt, or a banana there?

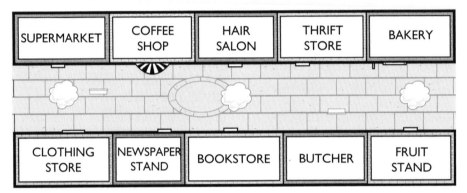

| SUPERMARKET | COFFEE SHOP | HAIR SALON | THRIFT STORE | BAKERY |

| CLOTHING STORE | NEWSPAPER STAND | BOOKSTORE | BUTCHER | FRUIT STAND |

JUNK FOOD JUMBLE

A burger, some fries, an ice cream, and a thick vanilla shake—they're so unhealthy, yet so tasty.

Fill in the blank boxes so that each row and each column in the grid has only one of each junk food item.

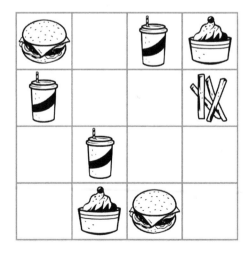

WHAT'S DIFFERENT?

The monkeys from the local zoo have escaped and invaded the supermarket. Can you find the ten differences between these two pictures of mayhem?

BUILD YOUR OWN SUMMER SPACE ROCKET

Rockets are really simple machines—just a tube filled with fuel, a nose cone, and some fins. The fuel makes air rush out of the bottom end, and the nose cone and fins help the tube to fly straight as it shoots into the air!

You will need:

a fizzy aspirin or vitamin C tablet • a film canister with lid • scissors • a piece of thin cardstock • adhesive tape

PREPARING FOR LAUNCH

1. Cut out the shapes opposite using a pair of scissors. You may want to ask an adult for help.

2. Give your rocket a name that is out of this world and write it on the circle, avoiding the shaded quarter.

3. Cut the shaded quarter out of the circle, and tape the straight edges together to form a cone.

4. Place the film canister on the long edge of the piece of cardstock and roll the paper up to make a tight tube. Secure it in place using tape as shown with the lid at the bottom.

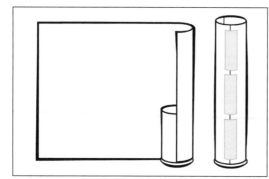

5. Attach the cone to the top of your rocket using tape.

6. Fold the four fins along the dotted lines and then tape the folded edges to the base of your rocket as shown.

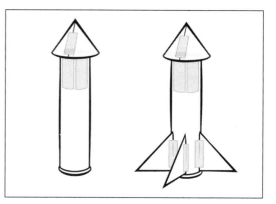

6...5...4...3...2...

7. Now you are ready to launch your rocket. Turn it upside down and take the lid off the canister. Fill the canister two-thirds full of water. Then drop in half a fizzy tablet and quickly replace the lid.

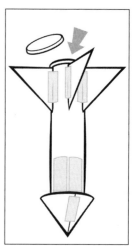

Cut out the pieces below and fold along the dotted lines.

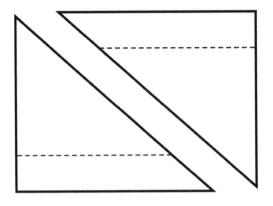

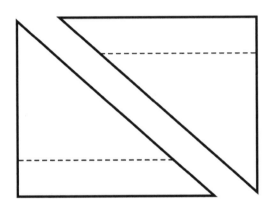

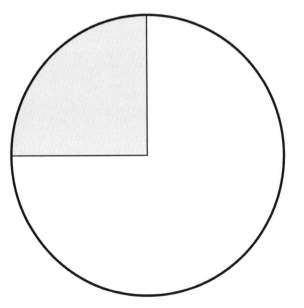

8. Put your rocket back the right way up, stand back, and wait for blast-off! (Note: You may want to launch your rocket outside since water will come out of it.)

Tip: Make more than one rocket and have a competition to see which rocket shoots the highest. Experiment with different shapes of cone and fin to see if these will give your rocket the edge against the competition.

Doodle the launching rocket.

Back of the rocket.

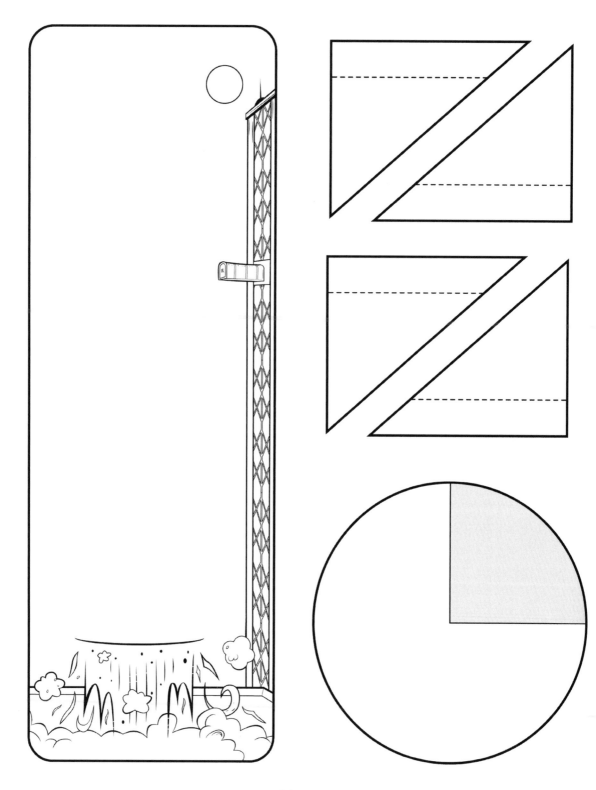

SUMMER AT THE THEME PARK

Can you find your way around the rides at the theme park?
Check your answers on page 96.

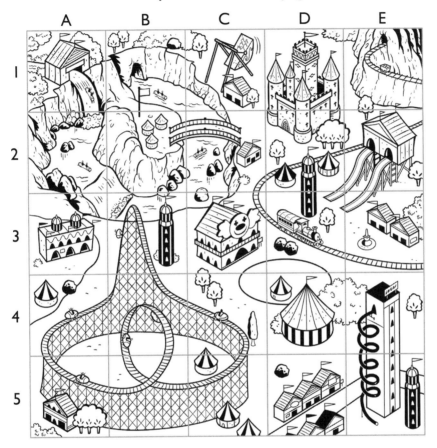

Start at the square indicated by the number and letter in parentheses. Then find your way around the park following the directions and using the compass below.

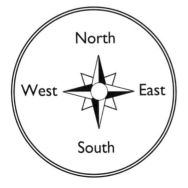

Example: The Giant Swing (**1C**). If you go 2 squares south, 2 east, 2 south, 1 west, and 1 north, you end up at the Big Top (**4D**).

1. Starting from the Spiral Slide (**5E**):

    2 north, 2 west, 1 south, 1 east

2. Starting from the Rickety Bridge (**2C**):

    2 south, 2 west, 3 north

3. Starting from the Coaster (**5A**):

    2 north, 4 east, 1 north

THE ULTIMATE SUMMER PENTATHLON

A pentathlon is an athletic competition made up of five events. When the sun is shining, go to the park and hold your own pentathlon. You will need at least three players. The player who wins the most events is the ultimate champion.

EVENT ONE: The Standing Long Jump

Mark a line on the grass using some string. Take turns standing behind the line, and jump as far as you can over the line without a running start. Mark where you land with a twig. The person who jumps the farthest is the winner.

EVENT TWO: The Ping-Pong Put

This event is like the shot put—players throw a heavy metal ball as far as they can. In this event, you must use a ping-pong ball. Hold the ball in the palm of your hand level with your jaw. Push your arm forward as strongly as you can and release the ball—the person who throws the farthest is the winner.

EVENT THREE: Puff Ball

Mark two lines on the ground, roughly nine feet apart. Ask each player to place his ping-pong ball on the first line, and kneel down behind it. You must race to get your ping-pong ball from the first line to the second and back again using only the power of your puff. The first to reach the finish line is the

EVENT FOUR: The High Jump

Two players hold a length of rope or string between them, keeping it very low to the ground. The jumper must jump over the rope. If he manages it, the rope is raised higher off the ground to make the jump more challenging. The person who can jump the highest, wins.

EVENT FIVE: Target Bowls

Drop a tennis ball on the ground and take two large steps away. Mark this spot with a stone. Each player should kneel by this stone and roll a ping-pong ball toward the tennis ball. The goal is to get as close to the tennis ball as possible without touching it. The player that rolls his ball closest to the tennis ball is the winner.

Oh no! What is the shot put going to land on?

WORLD MENU MADNESS

Solve these menu muddles and then check
your answers on page 96.

MEATBALL MAYHEM

How many meatballs can you find in the Italian restaurant?

WHERE IN THE WORLD?

Link the countries to their delicious delicacies. The first one is done for you.

Lasagna	France
Jellyfish with noodles	Spain
Grilled guinea pig	Italy
Frogs' legs	Indonesia
Frankfurter	Peru
Bat stew	United Kingdom
Tortilla	China
Toad in the hole	Germany

Draw the ultimate ice-cream sundae.

THE SUMMER OF FUN

Keep a record of your summer of fun by drawing, sticking, or painting pictures of all the exciting things you have been doing this summer.

ALL THE ANSWERS

SUMMER SPACE GETAWAY
pages 4 and 5

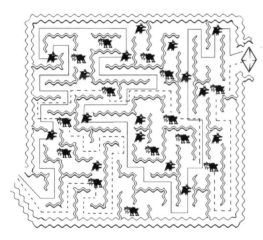

To the crystal: ——————

To the spacecraft: ------------

ANCHORS AWAY!
page 7

1. C, 2. A, 3. B

AWESOME ANIMAL QUIZ
pages 8 and 9

1. A, 2. B, 3. B, 4. B, 5. D, 6. C, 7. D, 8. A, 9. C, 10. B, 11. A, 12. B

BOX CLEVER
page 12

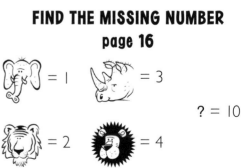

INVESTIGATE THE CRIME SCENE
pages 15 and 16

1. A; 2. Planet Earth and the Sphinx in Egypt; 3. On the pillow; 4. At the foot of the bed; 5. Closed; 6. On the right; 7. A; 8. One; 9. Open; 10. A

FIND THE MISSING NUMBER
page 16

elephant = 1   rhino = 3

? = 10

tiger = 2   lion = 4

PUZZLE PARK
pages 18 and 19

J loves the slide and the swings, but does not like the merry-go-round or laying on the grass.

ORANGE, BANANA, RASPBERRY, STRAWBERRY, CHOCOLATE, PEACH

Chocolate—the rest are fruits.

Squirrels **C** & **H**

WORLD SPORTS CHALLENGE
page 25

Cristiano Ronaldo – Soccer – Portugal
Lewis Hamilton – Race Car Driving – Great Britain
Roger Federer – Tennis – Switzerland
Tiger Woods – Golf – USA
Jose Canseco – Baseball – Cuba
Usain Bolt – Track & Field – Jamaica
Ian Thorpe – Swimming – Australia

PICTURE PUZZLER
page 24

WHAT'S DIFFERENT?
page 28

ISLAND DISCOVERY
page 29

I. 12; **2.** 5; **3.** West; **4.** A lighthouse;
5. A swimming pool; **6.** 6

CODE BREAKER
page 30

One: THE FILES ARE IN THE FRIDGE.

Two: GIVE THEM TO MY MOM.

Three: TELL MOM I WANT HOT DOGS FOR DINNER.

1. The files are cold.
2. Hot Dogs.

ISLAND ADVENTURES
page 33

A = Bananas   **B** = Coconuts

CROSSED WIRES
page 35

Plug **A** = Robobutler.
Plug **B** = Chocotoaster.
Plug **C** = Instajellymatic.

MESSAGE IN A BOTTLE
page 43

1. "Congratulations! You have won a free ice cream!"

2. The alphabet is spelled out backward again. "Present these messages at Joe's Café to claim . . ."

3. Color in the squares matching the numbers by each row. Then read the leftover letters. "A glass of homemade lemonade."

TENT TROUBLE
page 45

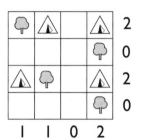

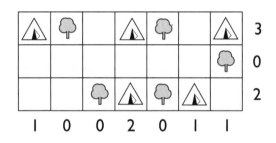

ROLLER-COASTER RIDE
pages 46 and 47

Area **K**

Ron is the man with the beard in the second row.

HIT THE BEACH
page 49

SUMMER AT THE CIRCUS
pages 52 and 53

Box **C**

Nine feet further away and six feet to the right

F2, **F3**, **C5**, and **D4**

Ball 14

HIGH-FLYING HANJIE
page 57

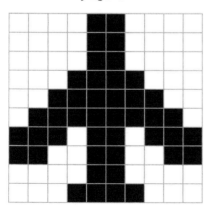

TREASURE HUNT
page 67

ROAD TRIP
page 70

Trip A: New York; Washington, DC; Miami; Dallas; Los Angeles.
Trip B: Seattle; Minneapolis; Chicago; Denver; Las Vegas.
Trip C: Las Vegas; Los Angeles; Dallas; Washington, DC; New York.

You have not visited San Francisco, Kansas City, or Indianapolis.

PUZZLE CITY
page 72

Bangkok, Thailand; New Delhi, India; Beijing, China; Madrid, Spain; Moscow, Russia; Berlin, Germany; Paris, France; Washington, DC, USA; Canberra, Australia

Garage **C**

CARS, PLANES, AND TRAINS
pages 74 and 75

A + F, B + D, C + G, E + I; H is unique.

Kit **B**

H8, B4, and J2

DOWN ON THE FARM
pages 76 and 77

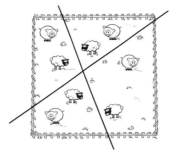

SUMMER FUN ON MAIN STREET
pages 80 and 81

Newspaper stand, fruit stand, banana

SUMMER AT THE THEME PARK
page 85

1. The Big Top (**4D**); **2.** Thunder River (**1A**); **3.** The Slip and Slide (**2E**)

WORLD MENU MADNESS
page 88

Thirty meatballs

Lasagna – Italy
Jellyfish with noodles – China
Grilled guinea pig – Peru
Frogs' legs – France
Frankfurter – Germany
Bat stew – Indonesia
Tortilla – Spain
Toad in the hole – United Kingdom